IMAGES
of America

WILMINGTON

Wilmington is viewed from Boyd Hill around the late 1800s. Haystack Mountain rises in the distance (left), while the hills feature wide open pastures, a product of widespread farming and logging. There are glimpses of what is now Route 9 (middle distance, right of center) as well as Ray Hill Road (far distance, on far right). There is even a puff of steam from a train leaving the station (middle distance, to the left of center). A number of these buildings still exist today. (Courtesy of the Historical Society of Wilmington.)

ON THE COVER: Looking west down Main Street, during a time before automobile traffic, as traces of wagon wheels cross the iron bridge built in 1888. In the distance, Haystack Mountain peers over the horizon. Across the bridge on the riverbank sits A.L. Childs & Son Store—known today as Dot's Restaurant. In the foreground, behind the book's spine wraparound, are the porches of William Avery's store prior to it becoming the well-known Bank Building. (Courtesy of the Historical Society of Wilmington.)

IMAGES
of America

WILMINGTON

Julie Moore and Nathan Moore

ARCADIA
PUBLISHING

Published by Arcadia Publishing
Charleston, South Carolina

Printed in the United States of America

Library of Congress Control Number: 2019957283

For all general information, please contact Arcadia Publishing:
Telephone 843-853-2070
Fax 843-853-0044
E-mail sales@arcadiapublishing.com
For customer service and orders:
Toll-Free 1-888-313-2665

Visit us on the Internet at www.arcadiapublishing.com

*To all past Wilmingtonians who saw the need to document and
preserve the history of their town so as to educate, enlighten, and
inspire future Wilmingtonians. This book could not exist without you.*

CONTENTS

ACKNOWLEDGMENTS

The process of delving into Wilmington's history and learning the little details of the town's past has been very rewarding. Uncovering rare photographs and reading centuries old stories about the people and places in the town where we both grew up was well worth the experience. Physically seeing images of buildings demolished long ago, merry fairgoers socializing on the ball fields, raging floodwaters gushing through town, and past Old Home Week parades marching down Main Street—all captured in slices of time—has been eye-opening to say the least. The deeds and memories of those long gone have left their marks on Wilmington, whether we are aware of it or not.

This book is the result of the dedication of those who took the time to preserve a part of Wilmington's past. A tremendous thank you goes to past Wilmingtonians who saw the need to take a photograph, write down memories, save a newspaper article, or rescue a piece of memorabilia in order to one day help retell Wilmington's history; this book would not exist without their foresight! Among those past Wilmingtonians we wish to thank are Ralph Medbury, Porter Thayer, Phil Stapleton, Olive Buffum, Mary Maynard, Phil Smyth, Guy Hawkins, Phil Ware, Barbara Look, Margaret Greene, Janet Pool, Evelyn Keefe, Viola Morse, Rita Staib, John Taft, Eugene Sullivan, and Jay Canedy.

We would also like to thank everyone who answered a question, provided a photograph, or simply voiced their words of encouragement along the way. Unfortunately, space does not allow the inclusion of everyone's names, but there are some who went above and beyond to help us document Wilmington's history prior to the mid-1960s: the Historical Society of Wilmington curator Harriet Maynard, Bob LeBlond, Bill and Sharon Adams, the Brattleboro Historical Society, the *Brattleboro Daily Reformer*, Linda Stapleton Olsson, Frank Merrick, Will Melton, Wes Ives, Claudia Greene, Pat Crawford Morris, Betsy Ray Myers, Walter White, Larry Chase, Spencer Crispe, Wilmington Works, and the descendants of Martin A. Brown.

And thank you especially to our readers: We hope you enjoy this glimpse into Wilmington's past—perhaps even while reading this you are standing where history was made!

All images are courtesy of the Historical Society of Wilmington, unless otherwise indicated.

INTRODUCTION

As with many New England towns of the time, Wilmington was founded by Benning Wentworth, then governor of New Hampshire. The original land grants were issued on April 29, 1751, with 64 equal shares of land divided amongst 59 people, along with allotments for a minister, a school, and a church. Settlers began to arrive slowly, and by December 1765, it was reported that seven families were living in the area, with several more beginning the process of clearing and improving their land. Wilmington's population quickly blossomed to a 19th-century high of 1,369 in 1820 before leveling off to around 1,250 in 1900.

Wilmington's early settlers were clearly a brave and hardy bunch, choosing to face the danger and hardship of pioneer life in order to stake out their livelihoods in the stone-bound forests of the Green Mountains under the threat of rigorous winter weather. The original village was constructed atop Lisle Hill, owing to land better suited for bearing crops and the ability to more quickly detect approaching threats.

As the town's population began to grow, residents banded together, holding logging and husking bees, apple parings, quiltings, and structure raisings. It could take as many as 20 men to heave the big timbers into place when raising a barn or other structure. The early settlers often combined work with social functions. While the men logged or raised buildings, the women would prepare dinners on long tables loaded down not just with potatoes, corn, or game, but also with pies, donuts, cakes, apples, cider, and rum to reward all for a hard day's work. Such functions usually ended with a rowdy game of forfeits, in which friends and neighbors challenged each other to silly and outrageous stunts such as standing on one's head, dancing a jig, or hopping around on one leg.

Being among the first settlers to the area, there were no mills in the village and little in the way of maintained roads to use for extensive travel. As such, when it came time to transport their grain to the mills, Wilmington's first settlers were forced to carry the grain on horseback or often even their own backs to the mills in Brattleboro. The trip was about 20 miles over the hills, or even farther if traveling through the valleys. At that time, many of these same settlers served as carriers for Wilmington's mail. With no regular carrier service until the late 1700s, the mail was essentially moved by anyone who happened to be coming to or leaving from Wilmington. By 1800, there was a post office on the common, and by 1896, Rural Free Delivery had come to Vermont, providing more regular delivery for everyone.

As both Wilmington and the surrounding villages grew, mills began to be erected in the valley, with the first going up in 1784, inspiring the name Mill Hollow. By 1828, a new government highway had been constructed, which ran through Mill Hollow on its way between Bennington and Brattleboro. Soon the economic opportunities brought by increased traffic through town had caused several other structures to pop up in Mill Hollow—the first being a wheelwright shop, which was soon followed by a small hotel.

The town meeting held in 1833 brought a vote wherein the townspeople decided to move all future town meetings to Mill Hollow, along with procuring a contract for a meetinghouse to hold them in. Businesses also began relocating to Mill Hollow, and soon most of the village had been picked up and moved to the valley via oxcarts. Wilmington quickly became a great cattle center. Fairs were attended by farmers from miles around who wished to see and buy good stock for their own farms. A team of "Wilmington oxen" was treated like the equivalent of a blue-ribbon team at a modern horse show. Trades began to flourish, and outsiders started to flock to town, using it as a hub to seek their fortunes in cities like Boston and New York. Wilmington, Vermont, was now officially on the map.

Wilmington's reputation as a country town where city folks could escape the hustle and bustle of urban life was bolstered when the railroad finally reached town on November 4, 1891. Connecting Wilmington to Readsboro, North Adams, Massachusetts, and beyond, the advent of the railroad helped to boost not only the tourism trade in Wilmington, but also the growing sawmill and pulp mill industry centered around Mountain Mills. Mountain Mills' sawmill alone had an output of 50,000 board feet per day and seven million board feet per year. Every spring during the thaw, log drivers transported logs down the Deerfield River from logging camps in Searsburg, Somerset, Glastenbury, and Dover to the 75-acre holding pond above the mills.

At that same time, booming tourism supported the creation of hotels and "resorts," such as the Hotel Raponda, which attracted numerous out-of-state visitors. For many years, families from the cities would spend their summers at the hotel, enjoying recreational activities at the lake as well as the quiet country atmosphere. Visitors to inns like the Vermont House enjoyed fine dining, electricity, and stables where horses could be rented or sightseeing trips on horse-drawn carriages could be arranged. Wealthier visitors might also opt to join a club, such as the Forest & Stream Club, where members could hike, fish, hunt, and enjoy a lively social atmosphere. As cars became more common, visitors passing through town could spend a night at the Haystack Cabins and enjoy the quiet solitude of country evenings. Among Wilmington's more famous visitors were former presidents Theodore Roosevelt, Grover Cleveland, and Rutherford B. Hayes (whose mother, Sophia Birchard, was born in Wilmington in 1792), along with writer Rudyard Kipling. Kipling, in particular, was said to be fascinated by logging and lumbermen and once requested that lumberman Joseph Gilbert float a log out onto Lake Raponda to demonstrate how the log drivers rode the logs during the spring drives—much to Kipling's delight.

As Wilmington grew, so too did its sense of community. Social clubs, fairs, community organizations, and charitable groups sprang up, allowing both new and old residents to socialize, share memories, and support causes such as Wilmington troops fighting overseas. Even many residents who moved away took a piece of Wilmington with them. In 1890, on the front porch of the Vermont House, a group of residents met to plan a family reunion. Eventually it was decided to expand the reunion to include the entire town—with even former residents who had since moved away being invited back to participate in the event. Held in July 1890, the Reunion of the Sons and Daughters of the Town of Wilmington, now known as Old Home Week, ushered in a beloved and enduring tradition. For every decade since, Wilmington has held a reunion of residents past and present filled with events such as class reunions, picnics, sporting matches, speeches, remembrances, exhibitions, and parades.

Believed by many to be the first of its kind, Wilmington's Old Home Week has stood the test of time and truly encapsulates Wilmington's most enduring quality as a place where residents both old and new can thrive in a close-knit community of neighbors, friends, and family.

One

WILMINGTON'S STEADFAST LANDMARKS

An unidentified man stands at the site of the old village established on Lisle Hill. In 1828, a government road between Bennington and Brattleboro was built through Mill Hollow, where Wilmington's mills were located. By 1833, the town had voted to begin holding town meetings in Mill Hollow rather than in the original village, with most of the town eventually being moved down the hill via oxcart that same year.

Opening in 1880 and seen here during Old Home Week 1960, this building housed the O.O. Ware Store, post office, and Masonic Lodge. Famed for his maple products, which shipped across the United States and Europe, Orrin O. Ware's syrup was entered in the 1893 World's Columbian Exposition in Chicago, winning a gold medal. A popular meeting place for locals, the store also sold fresh meats, clothing, and boots.

Born in 1847, Orrin O. Ware (pictured) was a leading Wilmington merchant. Gaining business experience starting at the age of 12, Ware later opened his own store in 1880. Ware recalled that during World War I, his storefront would become packed as townspeople awaited the midnight stagecoach carrying letters from local soldiers. Ware also served as postmaster in Wilmington for about 20 years. (Courtesy of Bob Ware.)

The present town hall is pictured during Old Home Week 1890 (above) and again during the 1950s (right). It was the fourth such building constructed in Wilmington. The first two town halls were on the original town common, while the third, deemed to be of inferior quality, was torn down to make way for the fourth. Completed in 1879, it hosted its first town meeting later that year and has experienced many renovations, including seeing the second floor raised by two feet and a bay window added. Upstairs was used for doctors' offices and other businesses and even hosted basketball games for a time. For a period between the late 1800s and the 1960s, the post office was also housed here. Town meetings eventually outgrew this building and were moved to Memorial Hall. (Above, courtesy of Linda Olsson.)

Famous for its soda fountain, Parmelee & Howe was a popular place for locals to congregate. Charles Parmelee traded his farm for the original wood building (front, left) in the fall of 1888. Parmelee ran the store himself until 1916 when Ralph Howe Sr. became a partner, officially changing the name to Parmelee & Howe. Seen here prior to 1903, the original building burned down in 1931 and was later replaced by the present brick structure. During reconstruction, the store operated out of what is now Dot's Restaurant. The flood of 1938 heavily damaged the store, but, after debris and old merchandise were removed, the store was reopened once again. In 1951, management changed again with Ralph Howe Jr. and Leonard "Pete" Johnson taking over. The store expanded in 1960 to sell hardware and sporting goods, remaining a landmark establishment in Wilmington until its closure in 1994.

Seen here during Old Home Week 1960, the Old Bank Building was purchased by the Wilmington Savings Bank in 1885. Established in 1853, the bank spent several years without a building or vault; its treasurer S.P. Flagg carried the assets in his vest pocket! The bank moved out in 1970, leaving the vault alarm box behind. In 2007, the building was destroyed by fire, forever changing the look of Wilmington.

After merging with other banks in 1935, the now Vermont Savings Bank completed an interior renovation in 1956. The bank held an open house to show off the new interior along with a display of bank records dating back to the very first deposit of $10 in 1854. From left to right are clerks Leonard Brown, Bertha Jacobs, and Dorothy Vogel. (Courtesy of the Brattleboro Historical Society.)

An iconic view during Old Home Week 1910 shows Childs Tavern (center, now Crafts Inn), with its luxurious front porch, flanked by the Times Building (left) and Memorial Hall (right). The *Deerfield Valley Times* was established as Wilmington's local newspaper in 1888. The original Times Building burned down in 1891. By 1892, the structure was rebuilt, and the paper continued until 1942. Childs Tavern, built in 1898, was designed by the same architectural firm that designed

Memorial Hall, itself built in 1902 to honor Maj. F.W. Childs and Wilmington's servicemen. The tavern was sold to Floyd Crafts Sr. in 1911, and by 1921, the Childs family had chosen to sell Memorial Hall as well. It was turned over to the town for $8,000 and the stipulation that a memorial service be conducted there annually—a tradition still observed today.

The Norton House (pictured) is believed to be one of the oldest remaining structures from the original town common, dating back to 1760. Constructed in the Cape Cod style, it was moved to Mill Hollow via oxcart. The building features many original accoutrements, such as hand-hewn beams, wide board floors, handmade glass windows, three fireplaces feeding a central chimney, and the original baking oven. A large barn from the 1800s existed in the rear up until its destruction in the flood of 1938. The original barn door is still present inside the remaining building. Now a retail and sewing shop, Mildred Norton and her mother, Martha, previously operated a hat shop in the parlor of the building until it was sold to the present owner. The building was again heavily damaged in the flood of 2011, though it has since been restored.

Tourists on horse and buggies line up in front of the Vermont House, ready for sightseeing. Constructed in 1850, the Vermont House remains an inn to this day. At the turn of the 20th century, owner Frank Allen had the inn modernized with electric lights and steam heat. The livery stable housed horses available for guests staying in the inn's 35 rooms. Allen's sister May Crafts oversaw table service. Her cuisine was lauded for using real yellow cream, fine butter, fresh eggs, and pure maple syrup—all locally produced. Allen, well-known for his knowledge of the valley, took great pleasure in introducing guests to nearby points of interest. For this reason, his inn became a popular rendezvous point in Wilmington, catering to commercial travelers, newspapermen, contractors, blacksmiths, doctors, and even locals. The inn's dining room was said to be often jolly but always civil.

Before becoming the iconic Dot's Restaurant in 1958, this building (front, left, shown with curb service stand) had many uses. From the late 1800s into the early 1900s, it was A.L. Childs & Son Store, featuring a soda fountain that sold homemade ice cream using eggs and cream from local farms. In 1931, after a fire, Parmelee & Howe briefly occupied the building. During the 1930s, it was the first home of Ray Corkin's Green Shutters restaurant. For a while it was the Deerfield Dairy Bar, one of several popular lunch counters in town; the interior is shown below in 1948. Since then, the building spent many years as Dot's Dairy Bar and later the more well-known Dot's Restaurant. Much of the original structure was lost after damages during the 2011 flood, though the restaurant has been rebuilt at the original site. (Below, courtesy of Frank Merrick.)

This view is looking south at what was then called River Street during Old Home Week 1910. The building on the right, bedecked in flags, was the Bowker Block. The streets were quieter and emptier in a time with few cars. Note the dirt streets lined with wagon wheel tracks and the lack of traffic controls or speed limit signs. (Courtesy of the Porter Thayer Collection.)

Known as the Pulsifer Block, this building was one of the original structures constructed on the old town common and moved to Mill Hollow in 1833. On Lisle Hill, the building was occupied by Dr. Billings Pulsifer. The block has been home to many businesses over the years, including a restaurant (seen here), a grocery store, a jewelry store, and a photography shop.

This view is looking east in 1916 down what is now Route 9, across from the local supermarket. In the far distance is the recently built White House Inn, then a home named Beaver Brook. Today, the area has seen heavy development. The Catholic church now resides on the left side of the road, and many homes and businesses fill the once wide-open spaces.

The Newton House was owned by James Newton, a financier and partner in the Newton Brothers' local businesses, which included a railroad and a lumber company. Newton enjoyed southern Vermont enough to purchase this summer home in Wilmington. The home was sold to Martin Brown in 1912. Brown eventually removed the house to build Beaver Brook, which is now the well-known White House Inn. (Courtesy of the Newton family.)

Along with Beaver Brook, Brown also built a smaller house across the street named The Playhouse (seen here from Beaver Brook). The Playhouse was used by Brown's children, and as a roadside tearoom where passing motorists could buy ice cream, sandwiches, salads, and tea. It is said that famous bandleader Paul Whiteman once visited the tearoom for lunch while passing through Wilmington in the 1920s.

Finished in 1916, Beaver Brook became the Browns' summer home. Brown's wife, Clara, loved entertaining guests here, and it is rumored that her ghost still makes appearances at the home. A full-sized bowling alley, popular with Brown's grandchildren, occupied the basement. After its sale in 1964, the house was converted into an inn, utilizing the grand rooms for formal functions like weddings, and became known as the White House Inn.

The Averell Stand, built in 1820 by James Averell and his son Benjamin, was a well-known tavern and stagecoach stop on the road between Brattleboro and Bennington. Stationed nearby the Averell Stand was a schoolhouse that served District No. 3. The property was purchased by Martin Brown in 1912 and eventually became home to the Browns after their sale of the Beaver Brook property. (Courtesy of Larry Chase.)

Residents stand for a photograph near the Averell Stand at what is now known as the intersection between Route 9 East and Route 100 South. The Averell Stand School can be seen in the background. Travelers of the time used this intersection to navigate to Brattleboro, Jacksonville, or Colrain, Massachusetts.

The Shafter Street House was originally built in the shape of an octagon by Oscar Lovell Shafter in the 1840s. Shafter was an attorney and avid abolitionist who had recently graduated from Harvard Law School and settled in Wilmington around 1836 in order to practice law. During that time, Shafter became a member of the state legislature and purchased the land around the Shafter Street House after his marriage in 1840. The octagonal home eventually became a stop on the Underground Railroad. Slaves traveling towards Canada for freedom recognized the oddly shaped building as a place where they could seek refuge during their journey. The cupola at the top of the octagon was Shafter's personal sanctuary and study—friends and townspeople considered it a great honor to be invited into the cupola. In 1854, Shafter left Wilmington to practice law in California, going on to become an associate justice for the Supreme Court of California.

Pettee Memorial Library was built in 1906 with a Colonial Revival motif and named in memory of lifelong Wilmington residents Dr. Anson Pettee and his wife. The custom drinking fountain in front of the library (below), designed to be used by both people and horses, consists of a single seven-ton block of granite. The block was hauled from the railroad to the library by a pair of draft horses and put into place without the use of any derrick appliances. Prior to the Pettee Memorial Library, residents utilized what were known as "social libraries." Books were housed in both the post office and town hall as well as in private collections, and patrons could purchase special memberships granting access to various collections of books. The new library provided book lovers with a central location to find new books and information.

Two

SCHOOLING

Students stand before the Village School of District No. 2 during the 1890s. Until 1893, Wilmington was divided into school districts that served students in specific parts of town. Schoolhouses were shaped by the various populations they served, with as many as 16 districts operating in town during some years. The Village School originally stood where Pettee Memorial Library now sits, before being moved to where the firehouse now stands.

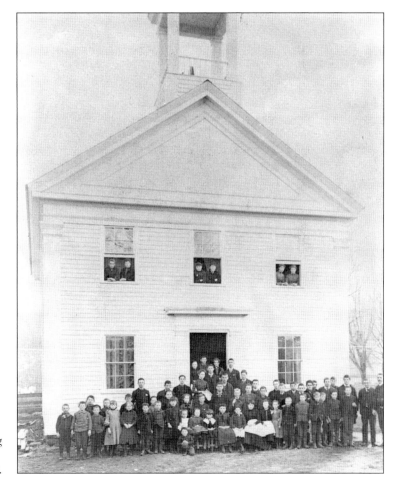

The Dix one-room schoolhouse of District No. 1 was located at the corner of Jacksonville Road and Ward's Beach Road. Like many buildings in rural Vermont, this school came to be known after the property nearby—in this case the property owned by the Dix family. This school was rebuilt in 1895, eventually turning into a residence before being destroyed in a fire.

Many of the old schoolhouses received second lives as residences or businesses. The smaller building seen here was once the Lawton School, located on Stowe Hill Road, which was part of District No. 5. The schoolhouse was purchased and later attached to Misty Mountain Lodge in the late 1950s (shown here) and used as guest rooms. (Courtesy of the Lensey Cole family.)

Pictured is a souvenir presented to students of the Corbett School of Wilmington's District No. 6 in 1899 by their teacher, Edna Haskell. This school was later known as Cold Brook School (below) and was moved from its original location in a meadow south of Cold Brook Bridge, where it was built in 1868. District schools were meant to serve pupils who lived outside the village and for whom daily travel to town for school would be difficult. In 1882, Wilmington had 27 teachers spread throughout 13 districts. A teacher's average salary was $57.97 per year, often coupled with free room and board provided by families residing within the district. Teachers would either rotate from family to family, or districts might put housing out to bid, with the lowest bidding family hosting that district's teacher for the year.

A teacher and her six pupils stand before the Cutting School of District No. 10, originally known as Upper Intervale School. In those days, a teacher was responsible not just for teaching a wide range of students, often ranging from four to 21 years old, but also for other tasks around the school. They would make sure the woodstove was going in the morning and do any required janitorial work around the classroom. A teacher might also be called upon to ready the schoolhouse as a gathering space for various neighborhood meetings and get-togethers. Students were generally responsible for their own lunches and would either return home to eat or, depending upon the weather, bring their lunch to school in a "dinner pail." (Above, courtesy of Larry Chase; below, courtesy of Walter White–Porter Thayer Collection.)

UPPER INTERVALE SCHOOL.

Boys pose on the stoop of the Fitch one-room schoolhouse of District No. 11, located on Higley Hill Road. While the sizes of Wilmington's schoolhouses could vary according to the class sizes they served, many, especially those farther from the village, were simple one-room affairs. Some schoolhouses might serve only a handful of students, while others could see 30 to 40 pupils all packed into a single room. Wilmington resident Viola Bishop Morse recalled that the schoolhouse she attended was only about 17 feet by 17 feet in size. Teachers were often noted for their ability to instill order amongst their pupils of varying ages and grades, a skill that must have come in handy when teaching a throng of young children all crammed together in a small room.

The Central School, Wilmington's first high school, combined two district schools along with the Village School, creating a single centralized school that opened in 1899. Several extensions to the original structure have been added over the years, with a gymnasium and extra classrooms in 1930, followed by more classrooms and a larger gymnasium in the brick portion of the building in 1956.

Young boys line a bench outside the Central School during recess. Collared shirts, breeches, and knee-high socks were the norm back in the day. The spot these boys occupy was eventually used to construct the brick building for the gymnasium that served the school for many years.

Students line up to board the school bus at the Central School in 1948. During the days of district schoolhouses, many students would walk to school. In some cases, an older student might take a horse and buggy to school while stopping to pick up other classmates along the way. As schooling became more centralized, the town started providing free busing for students to get to school.

1948

Annual Report

Town School District

OF WILMINGTON, VERMONT

•

WILMINGTON SCHOOL BUS

An elementary school classroom at the Central School is pictured here. The era of one-room schools in Wilmington officially came to an end with the 1949–1950 school year, except for a brief period during the 1955–1956 school year when the Cutting School and the Grange Hall were reopened to grades three through six due to overcrowding. These grades eventually moved to the new brick section of the Central School in 1956.

This was the science classroom at the Central School. The curriculum was quite extensive upon first opening, featuring English, Latin, French, civil government, zoology, botany, geography, physics, astronomy, algebra, and various history classes. The school yearbook, *The Mirror*, was first published in 1921, and in 1923, the school was placed on the New England College Entrance approval list. By 1938, the school was rated one of the top 13 in the state.

Students play during recess at the Central School during the 1940s. Note several outbuildings in the distance, some of which still exist today and are used by the athletic department and the Deerfield Valley Farmers' Day Association. Boyd Hill can also be seen in the background with significantly fewer trees than today.

Three

A WAY OF LIFE

The Deerfield Valley Creamery Association formed in 1885 to manufacture creamery products using locally produced milk. In 1923, a record 129,571 pounds of butter was produced. During its peak, the creamery consisted of 100 farmers from Wilmington, West Dover, and Marlboro. Over time, many farmers switched to selling milk instead of creamery products, and by 1939, the charter was terminated. Pictured is the creamery's float from Old Home Week 1920.

In 1893, while still hard at work as a log driver and lumberman, Joseph Gilbert Jr. purchased the Chauncy Smith farm on The Dover Road, naming it Gilberthurst Farm (above). Gilbert also started a milk and cream business in 1908 after establishing his own milk route, delivering fresh dairy around town. Along with the milk route, Gilbert also ran a very popular livery service during the summer months, which was even utilized by writer Rudyard Kipling when he visited Wilmington. In 1928, while the barn (left) was packed with hay, lightning struck and burned the barn to the ground, leaving a large void on the farm. After retiring, Gilbert became an avid gardener and was quite proud of his flowers. Appropriately, lilacs have since taken over the old barn foundation. (Both, courtesy of Linda Olsson.)

From left to right, J. Burton Crafts, Charlotte Fiske, Richard Eaton, Ruth Crafts, Parsons Crafts, and Pliny Crafts are heading to town in 1909 along what is now Route 100. The calves are Durham shorthorns raised by Roswell Crafts on his Maplewood Farm. Crafts began the farm to breed better milking stock for New England farms. Maplewood Farm was very well-known for shipping quality stock around New England and New York.

In the 1800s, John Newton, of the Newton Brothers, owned Maplehurst Farm until his passing, after which Frank Mann purchased the farm. In 1931, Harold Wheeler bought the farm and later purchased the Haskell, Gilbert and Crafts farms, thus adding more farmland. Shown atop the hill was the Woffenden farm. The Wheeler farm is now the last operating dairy farm in Wilmington. (Courtesy of the Porter Thayer Collection.)

The Homer Fitch farm, along The Dover Road, had an elevated railway to cross the Deerfield River. There were 10 acres of farmland on one side of the river and another 27 acres on the other side. To access the property across the river, there was a foot bridge and the elevated railway that was built in the early 1930s (pictured). The railway was washed out during the 1938 flood.

Elm Tree Farm, owned and operated by A.D. Howe, was not your average cattle and sheep farm; here, they raised silver foxes! Howe would have as many as 15 foxes on the farm at one time. The farm was named after the beautiful elms that lined the front yard.

On February 1, 1947, tragedy struck on Adams Farm (above) when five-year-old Judy Adams vanished through the ice and into the Deerfield River while sliding with her friends. Help was summoned by ringing the bell at the sawmill, with volunteers from the community arriving quickly to search for the little girl. While the men searched the riverbanks, even venturing out onto the broken ice, the women gathered to brew and deliver coffee to the searchers. Unfortunately, the search proved difficult, and the body was not recovered until two months later when the river ice began to break up. The incident was one of many examples of Wilmington residents coming together to help neighbors in need. (Above, courtesy of Bill and Sharon Adams; right, courtesy of Larry Chase.)

With increasing automobile traffic through Wilmington, it was decided to purchase a rock crusher in 1925 in order to help level out the roads through town. As a teenager, Harold Howe was hired to pound rocks with a 12-pound hammer so they fit into the crusher. Screens separated the material into various sizes while a conveyor dumped the material into bins for loading onto trucks. (Courtesy of Larry Chase.)

The Fred May farm, also known as Valley Brook Farm, was located on Higley Hill. May was known as a progressive farmer who was a member and advocate for the Farm Bureau as well as the Deerfield Valley Farmers' Day Association. In 1941, barn fires destroyed 75 tons of hay, pieces of farm machinery, and two hogs. The original barns are pictured here. (Courtesy of Larry Chase.)

The original Haskell farmhouse (pictured) was built by Andrew Haskell and dates back to the early 1800s. The barn stands on the opposite side of the road, with Haskell Hill Road once being a part of the original farm. Several generations lived on the farm, with Herbert Haskell being the last Haskell resident, passing in 1958. Fire consumed the original house in 1993.

Alton and Bernice Cross originally owned a dairy farm that shipped milk. In the late 1950s, they stopped due to the cost of bulk milk tanks. This began a transformation into Cross Trailer Park: people stopped to ask if they could park their campers in the Crosses' field, and one-by-one, fueled by increasing ski traffic, trailers were added—eventually forming the park there today. (Courtesy of the Cross family.)

Edwin Boyd, knowing his farm would soon be under water at Mountain Mills, moved his family to this farm on July 4, 1923. It has been in the Boyd family ever since, with six generations working the land. They have raised both Durham and Holstein cows, along with other farm animals. Brushing in the fall was a popular pastime on the farm: brush was cut and then sold in bundles. Today, the brush is transformed into holiday decorations. Ernest "John" Boyd, shown below with his team of horses in July 1944, was a third-generation Boyd. He raised six children on the farm, one of whom, Daniel "Bucky" Boyd, still runs the farm today with his family. (Both, courtesy of the Boyd Family Farm.)

The Ralph May farm, also known as Windy Hill Farm, has resided in the May family for five generations, ever since being purchased by Samuel May from Elijah Howe in 1863. Located off Coldbrook Road, the farm sits across the way from the Wellman farm and affords great views of Haystack Mountain—some say the best in town. The farm gained its name from the refreshing, cool breeze that seems to be ever-present, even on the hottest of days. Historically, cows, sheep, and horses were kept here, with oxen being used before work horses became more commonplace. Maple sugaring season has always been an important time on the May farm, with sugaring being done on at least one sugar lot in most years and often even two sugar lots in some years. (Courtesy of Heidi Taylor.)

The Corbett farm, located in the northwest corner of Wilmington, is bisected by Coldbrook Road. Several generations of the Corbett family farmed this rugged land. The tidy farm with expansive stone walls was a sheep farm before becoming a dairy farm. In the early 1900s, when farmers were ready to sell their flocks, the animals were rounded up for a sheep drive to the train station and boarded for market.

Arthur Pinkam's High Mowing Farm was situated high on a hill looking out over the picturesque valley. Pinkham purchased the farm in 1941 from Harry Fox and started an elaborate Guernsey breeding farm. Pinkham had this replica covered bridge on Stowe Hill designed to resemble the Creamery Bridge in Brattleboro. The bridge provided reliable access to the farmland on the other side of the stream.

Sign painter Eleoda Maynard harrows the soil—another art. Maynard moved to Wilmington from Burlington to help at Arthur and Olive Buffum's farm on the backside of Castle Hill. Maynard and his wife, Mary Buffum, purchased the bordering farm (pictured above), raising their family there. Sugaring was a large part of their income, with most of the syrup made on the farm being sold to others. (Courtesy of Harriet Maynard.)

Off what is now Country Club Road was a slaughterhouse, owned and operated by George Streeter. At times, Streeter would have up to 100 young pigs on the farm, raising them for his meat market or to sell so other farmers could raise them. After Streeter passed away, Verne Adams bought the slaughterhouse and property and built Windswept Manor, shown here at right.

The above image features a scenic view of Wilmington coming over White House Hill, heading west on what is now Route 9. Note the barren hillside used for grazing farm animals. The only house in this valley that remains today is the first one on the left. At one time this was owned by Arthur Brown and later Harry Crawford. The large farm on the right, at the bottom of White's Road (shown below), was owned by the Canedy family. This unidentified man maneuvers a horse-drawn tedder around the field, getting hay ready for the barn. Martin Brown purchased the farm in the late 1920s and later had it torn down. (Both, courtesy of Deborah Canedy.)

This enormous, three-story barn was built in 1912 along the Molly Stark Trail at the Beaver Brook Farm, owned by Martin Brown. The construction of the barn was undertaken by the Terrill brothers. Brown raised registered Guernsey cattle and sold bottled milk on his dairy farm with farm manager Greeley Brown, his nephew, and later with Merrill Sheltra. Tragedy struck on February 8, 1957, when fire broke out, burning the barn to the ground. Help arrived from all over town, but only part of the herd could be saved. An overall view of Beaver Brook looking west is shown here, before the small house between the White House and the farmhouse was taken down and before the Playhouse was built.

The art of haying before modernized equipment is shown here on the Haslund farm, situated in southeast Wilmington. The farmhouse, built in the early 1800s, boasts many rooms, with four fireplaces and a baking oven. The Haslund family farmed for many years on this property and other neighboring farms, with one of the farms eventually becoming Molly Stark State Park. (Courtesy of Bruce and Barbara Cole.)

The Carner farm began in 1921 when Wayne and Grace Carner purchased land on Ray Hill. A house (pictured) was procured via the Sears mail-order catalog, and the farm was developed to sell milk from Jersey cows. The Carners' son Stanly delivered fresh milk straight to customers' refrigerators for 50 years, at first utilizing a horse-drawn delivery wagon (seen here) and later a truck. (Courtesy of Isabelle Hadley.)

The Fox farm, situated at the end of Aldrich Road, was built before 1832. Florence Fox, the last of the family to live on the farm, married Carl Howe in August 1924, and they continued farming the rugged land together. Having no children of their own, they sold the farm and moved to the village upon retirement. This was a common practice for many farmers. (Courtesy of Phyllis Maercklein.)

Francis and Hilda Minor began Hillside Poultry in 1938. Their son Dary purchased the business in 1960. The margin between the price of eggs and the cost of farming made for a challenge. Keeping the size of their flock consistent was important and keeping the overhead costs to a minimum kept the family business thriving until 1997 when the Minors retired. (Courtesy of Dary and Joan Minor.)

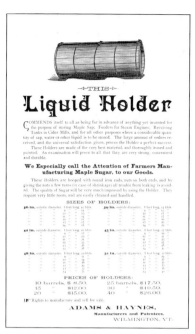

In 1865, Henry Adams purchased what is now Adams Farm. Adams and his friend Clinton Haynes invented, patented, and built liquid holders for storing maple sap (pictured). By the 1880s, a woodworking shop operated by a horse-powered treadmill was built to help meet the popular demand. While production ended in the 1940s, these tanks can still be seen across New England even today. (Courtesy of Bill and Sharon Adams.)

The Deerfield Valley Farmers' Exchange, incorporated in 1925, was another example of community. With the exchange, farmers were better able to market their product, get paid up front, and also become stockholders. On average, the farmers were supplying the exchange with 5,000 gallons of maple syrup per year. The exchange was located in the structure at right, with retail and office space in the Barber Building on Main Street.

Riverview Farm was home to Viola Bishop Morse growing up. The farm had a great sugar lot with an abundance of maple trees. Morse enjoyed sugaring season even as a young child, helping to scatter the buckets, gather sap, and even boil the sap down. Morse's father, Willie Bishop (shown here pouring syrup into the holding tank), had her start boiling sap at the age of 15.

Beaver Brook Sugar House was most likely the largest modernized sugar house in Wilmington when it was built in 1949. Owner Martin Brown was looking to develop the intersection across the way from the Averell Stand. Instead of the traditional wood-fired arch, Brown later designed the modernized arch to be heated with oil. In 1960, Robert Coombs purchased the operation and ran a very successful retail and gift shop business.

At one time, Wilmington had as many as 35 operating sugar houses. Sugaring went hand-in-hand with farming, and for some farmers this was the only cash crop they had. Shown here as a child is longtime sugar maker Henry Wheeler and his grandmother taking a break from gathering sap. Families would work the sugar lots together in order to cover the many tasks that sugaring entails. (Courtesy of Diane Wheeler.)

Shown here is George Crafts sugaring with a team of horses at the Titus farm on Ballou Hill Road in the spring of 1956. This location was the summer home of Ralph Titus and his wife for many years. Titus would hire sugar makers to run his sugar lot for him. The lot was well-known for its quality.

William Hall delivers meat to his customers in 1909. Hall raised beef cattle for wholesale and retail on his farm near Shearer Hill Road. His deliveries were an important part of living in the village where few farms raised beef cattle. Hall would also make weekly deliveries to logging camps deep in the woods of Somerset.

Logging and milling were once big business in Wilmington. Loggers spent the winter cutting and hauling logs from camps to river landings. Then, from March to mid-May, log drivers utilized the swollen rivers to drive logs downstream (pictured) to holding ponds at Mountain Mills. Bold log drivers jumped nimbly from log to log as they cascaded down the rivers, using peaveys and dynamite to guide the logs and break up dangerous jams.

In 1895, the Deerfield Lumber Company and the Newton Brothers built Mountain Mills, a large sawmill and pulp mill complex. The area rapidly filled with houses, stores, a hospital, a railroad station, and a school, becoming a town unto itself. The railroad (above) was instrumental in shipping the mills' products out of the region. The mills closed in 1920, and a dam was built by the New England Power Company in 1923, creating Harriman Reservoir. The flooding, which began in February 1924, claimed many farms. Olive "Gram" Buffum documented the flooding, which happened as follows: the Moore farm began flooding on April 9, and the Boyd farm on April 14, followed by Moore's barn and the Upton farm on April 16. Webster's farm (below) caught fire during the flood, burning up on April 15, and by April 29, the Upton farm had also succumbed.

Hoosac Tunnel & Wilmington Railroad, known as the "Hoot-Toot & Whistle," debuted in Wilmington on November 4, 1891. The railroad marked a very exciting time for Wilmington with greater travel and shipping opportunities. In 1923, the tracks were moved to higher ground before Mountain Mills was flooded. Heavy flooding in 1927 and 1936 also impacted the railroad, with the 1936 flood ending rail service to Wilmington for good.

All of these fine pelts on the Edwin Boyd farm at Mountain Mills were the result of hunting and trapping, an activity that was a way of life for many. Bounties were paid for some animals, and trappers would take an ear down to the town clerk's office for payment. The hides were then either sold or tanned for their own purposes. (Courtesy of the Eugene Sullivan family.)

One of Wilmington's first mills, built in 1788, was believed to be on the west side of the Deerfield River opposite the present-day mill. In 1828, members of the Waste family built a mill on the other side of the river that eventually became known as the Wilmington Grain & Lumber Company. In spring, the logs would pile up in this pond, backing up for some distance while waiting to be sawed at the mill. The four-foot pulp continued on its way over the dam to the pulp mill at Mountain Mills. Around 1904, the mill burnt, but it was soon rebuilt by the Choate Manufacturing Company. The flood of 1938 destroyed the dam, and that was the end of the mill. The structure was turned into a restaurant in 1939 by Verne Adams, and rooms were added in 1955. It is known today as the Old Red Mill. The building on the right was known as Fort Ashley and stood at the end of Gorham Lane.

Ludington Mill was built in 1914 by the Ludington Woodenware Company from Ludington, Michigan. The mill (above) churned out products such as clothespins, plywood trays for shipping butter and lard, wooden bowls, and bobbins for yarn, among other items. The mill was capable of producing over 600,000 clothespins in a single day. In November 1915, the mill burned to the ground, resulting in massive losses. However, it was soon rebuilt and eventually sold in 1928 to the New England Box Company, which was based in Greenfield, Massachusetts. The box factory (below) specialized in crafting banana and bread boxes. During World War II, the company produced wooden storage boxes for military equipment. In 1942 alone, the factory used over two million board feet of hardwood lumber. The introduction of waxed cardboard boxes caused the factory to shut down in 1963.

The Titus Mill (shown here) was an average-sized mill located just west of the Nutmeg Inn, along the Deerfield River. Among several owners over the years, Edward Titus used the property for a woodworking shop, and later Frank Bellows ran it as a sawmill. Logs shown in the yard were presumably shipped to the mill via the river. In the background is the Forest & Stream Club.

Brothers Oscar and John Howe were both blacksmiths and wheelwrights in Wilmington. Oscar's shop was originally on Depot Street (pictured at rear and to the right), and it is believed someone later moved the building to the bottom of Castle Hill (see page 48). John's shop, meanwhile, was located on Lisle Hill. Both brothers learned their trades from their father, Fayette Howe.

In 1868, John Buell and Stillman Robinson began a marble works business in Wilmington, across the bridge from the old bank building (pictured). The business worked both with various marbles found in Vermont and with foreign and domestic granites. In 1893, a tinsmith shop was built by A.L. Wheeler across the river from the marble works. Several houses on West Main Street were built specifically for the tinsmith workers.

Located across the street from Pettee Memorial Library (note the fountain), the Dixon House was home to prolific author and frequent *Saturday Evening Post* contributor Clarence Budington Kelland. Later, *Deerfield Valley Times* owner George Dixon operated his newspaper from the building. A victim of disrepair, the building was purchased by the town and demolished in 1973; this photograph was taken the day before the house was destroyed. (Courtesy of Deborah Canedy.)

H.F. Barber & Son Store, located on East Main Street in the village, sold rubber boots, shoes, and gentleman's furnishings, among other items. Ralph Medbury started working for Barber in 1907, earning 75¢ a day. Medbury purchased the business in 1922 and continued selling men's clothing. The local merchants regularly made time during their day to visit Medbury for a game of cribbage in the back storeroom.

Covey & Allen Furniture & Undertaking started in the original Times Building. Allen was the undertaker, with Covey running the store. They expanded their services by acquiring Buell's marble works in 1914 and the building adjacent the Masonic Hall in 1928. Covey (pictured) took over the business after Allen's death, later moving east on Route 9, where it is still located today. (Courtesy of Robert Covey Sr.)

In 1939, Ray Corkins built this gas station and gift shop next to his new Green Shutters restaurant on Route 9 East. In a prime location, tourists and locals alike filled their tanks and grabbed a bite to eat before hitting the road. Corkins sold the single-bay garage to Merrill Greene in 1941. Greene's son Robert purchased the business in 1963, and his son John still runs it today.

Louise Ray is standing in front of the service station her father, A.W. Ray, owned west of town. The photograph was taken in the early 1930s prior to the paving of the Molly Stark Byway. The small service station to the left of the Gulf pumps was later relocated behind the house and used as a summer cottage for Ray's wife, Corrine. (Courtesy of Betsy Myers.)

Guy E. Nido Sr. first started working in the oil business for Standard Oil Company. Traveling to Bennington, he would pick up an oil delivery before traveling back over the mountain to make deliveries with his horse-drawn sleigh. In 1913, several years after rail service came to Wilmington, fuel tanks were installed near the railyard (above). Below, Nido's delivery truck sits next to his barn on Ray Hill Road. In 1932, Standard Oil Company charged the village of Wilmington $111.75 for oiling the village streets to keep the dust to a minimum. By 1956, Nido had started his own business operating out of his Ray Hill home. After returning from the service, Guy E. Nido Jr. went to work for his father, eventually assuming ownership in 1968. (Below, courtesy of the Guy E. Nido Jr. family.)

Clarence Pike owned and operated a garage on this property until 1930. Roy Brown Sr. secured the Ford dealership that was previously operated by Leonard Brown from the Childs Tavern garage on West Main Street and moved it to this location. The first car sold at the new dealership was a 1930 Model A Ford coupe, shown above with Roy Brown Sr. In November 1950, a fire destroyed the entire garage during hunting season while the firemen were at camp. Brown quickly rebuilt a larger garage (shown below in 1958). The new four-bay garage had a showroom, office space, and gas pumps. Brown and his son Roy Brown Jr. ran Wilmington Garage Company, Inc., until 1961 when they held an auction and sold 21 vehicles. The site was sold to the Grand Union food chain, ending the Ford dealership era in Wilmington.

Antonia Mazelli stands behind the counter at Mazelli's Store. Mazelli and her husband, Guiseppe, immigrated to Vermont from northern Italy in the early 1900s, eventually buying a small grocery business in 1924. The store sold fresh fruit, vegetables, groceries, and sundries and also had a small lunch counter and ice cream parlor. The Mazellis' son Mario operated a home-to-home delivery service that sold fruits and vegetables. The younger Mazelli picked up produce in Albany, New York, and drove his fruit and vegetable truck on routes to Dover, Wardsboro, Jamaica, Whitingham, and Readsboro. The truck would also be parked on Main Street in Wilmington to sell produce. The store was eventually closed in 1934 when Grand Union took over the building that the Mazellis had been renting. (Above, courtesy of Nancy Harrison; below, courtesy of Bruce and Marcia Willard.)

Above sits Grand Union after the 1938 flood. Run by Harold Van Wyck and operated out of the building next to the Baptist church, it was a full-service establishment: items would be weighed out, taken to the counter, and costs tallied up by an employee. In some cases, employees had to use a long pole to retrieve items from the high shelving, like those behind the meat counter below. During the 1938 flood, attempts were made to place items on shelves as high as possible, but rapidly rising waters soon made that impossible. What little was salvageable, mainly canned goods, was put back up for sale in a temporary location while the main store was cleaned up. (Below, courtesy of David Hawkins.)

Beaton's Ranch House restaurant sat west of the village, situated between Vogel's farm and the District No. 8 schoolhouse. Kenneth and Burdys Beaton, who were former operators of the Dairy Bar in town, later built this fine new restaurant around 1954, serving up hot, fresh, home-cooked meals for weary travelers and locals alike. (Courtesy of the Brattleboro Historical Society.)

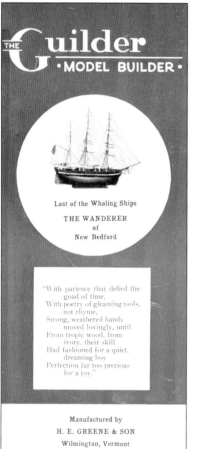

THE **Guilder** • MODEL BUILDER •

Last of the Whaling Ships
THE WANDERER
of
New Bedford

"With patience that defied the
goad of time,
With poetry of gleaming tools,
not rhyme,
Strong, weathered hands
moved lovingly, until
From tropic wood, from
ivory, their skill
Had fashioned for a quiet,
dreaming boy
Perfection far too precious
for a toy."

Manufactured by
H. E. GREENE & SON
Wilmington, Vermont

Catalogue 202

In September 1946, H.E. Greene and his son Kendrick assumed operations of the Guilder Model Builder business formerly owned and operated by Walter Guilder. The business, operating from a new building across from Haystack Cabins, was manufacturing and selling hobby equipment. After Greene passed in 1954, the business was sold to someone from out of state. George Schneeberger purchased the building in December 1957 and started G.S. Precision. (Courtesy of Don Greene.)

Four

CHURCHES AND
ORGANIZATIONS

First organized on the old town common in 1806, the Baptist congregation moved into its present building on Route 100 in 1839. The building was erected at a cost of $1,000. In 1928, the bell that once hung in the Methodist church was given to the Baptist church in order to replace its cracked bell. The bell remains at the Baptist church to this day.

Originally built near the Cutting-Intervale Cemetery in 1825 at a cost of $3,500, the Methodist church was moved to its present location in 1835. It is believed that the structure may have been moved on timbers with rollers pulled by oxen. Once at its new location, a steeple with belfry was added to the church. The bell, being the first in town, was purchased in Troy, New York, and drawn by oxcart to Wilmington. The bell called members to worship, alerted people of fires, and announced deaths in town. Deaths were announced with a few solemn strokes, followed by two quick strokes for a man and three for a woman. The deceased's age was then rung in groups of 10 strokes. In 1911, the structure was sold to the Masonic Social Lodge No. 38 F&AM, and the belfry was eventually removed in 1928. Lodge No. 38 was chartered in January 1857 but was not the first social lodge of Wilmington. The group still owns the building today. See page 110 for more history. (Courtesy of Robert Greene.)

The Universalist church building was erected in 1835 on land purchased for $60. The town clock and bell, a gift from the Childs family, were installed in 1890. In 1893, to pay off a $65 debt, each member was assigned to raise $1. This resulted in various, sometimes humorous, fundraising efforts, including a poetry reading by one member and another member who sold turnips door-to-door in a wheelbarrow.

In the early decades of the 1900s, the Universalist Ladies Aid organization put on church fairs in Memorial Hall. These events were popular with visitors and locals alike and featured elaborately decorated booths with homemade candy, food, needlework, aprons, braided rugs, and quilts. There was even a "mysterious grab bag" for youngsters. Eager customers especially enjoyed the tables filled with homemade ice cream and giant slices of cake.

After the original Congregational church (shown here) burned in 1882, plans for the present church were approved upon the condition that the costs not exceed $2,500. Stones for the foundation were drawn to the building site in 1883, with the entire structure being finished later that year. The church was outfitted with a pipe organ around 1915, and it remains today in what has now become the Episcopal church.

After the 1938 flood, Ray Corkins moved his restaurant, Green Shutters, from the site that is now Dot's Restaurant to a new building on Route 9 East. In May 1950, the Catholic Church purchased the new building. Services were held here until a new church could be built across the street. In 1965, the current Catholic church was completed, leaving the other building vacant for the Episcopal church to purchase.

Order of the Eastern Star (OES), Mayflower Chapter No. 19 was organized on April 22, 1913. The first year, 33 members were initiated into the chapter. OES is open to both men and women who wish to work together on projects for the benefit of others. Memorial Hall is shown here decorated for an OES district meeting held on September 17, 1951. Note the original stage curtain showing the bottom of Lisle Hill.

The Wilmington Red Cross Missionary Group is pictured at the Grand Army of the Republic Hall. From left to right are Minnie Barber, Juliet Adams, Mary Tripp, and Elsie Brown. This group, seen here folding bandages in 1918, helped the war effort by sending bandages, clothing, and medical supplies to US soldiers in Europe.

In order to promote US savings bonds, members of Wilmington's Nelson E. Pickwell Post of the American Legion stand aboard a flatbed truck as a replica of the Liberty Bell rolls through Wilmington in June 1950. From left to right are Eloff Johnson, Eleoda Maynard, and Leonard Boyd. Chartered in 1919, the post supports many community activities, including sponsoring Memorial Day services and placing flags on the graves of US soldiers.

Victory Grange No. 164, organized on January 15, 1875, is properly referred to as the "Patrons of Husbandry." The Grange was a way to include the farms as a community. One advantage for members was the financial savings from purchasing directly from producers. On October 16, 1947, the Grange purchased Oscar Howe's former blacksmith shop from the Deerfield Valley Farmers' Exchange, providing a spacious area for meetings and social functions.

In October 1915, village residents gathered, with C.B. Kelland presiding, to form a governing body for the newly organized YMCA. Five directors, one from each church denomination, were elected. Space was acquired at the old Choate Mill. Work was completed inside so the large room could be used as a gymnasium. Leagues were formed for basketball and indoor baseball. Younger members had the opportunity to use the facility also.

4-H Clubs, a great experience for boys and girls, promoted hands-on and leadership skills. The H's stand for head, heart, hands, and health. Wilmington had several of the clubs, including Flying Fingers, Garden, and Lassie's Sewing. Service projects, conducted yearly, included care of the property across from the Averell Stand. Members are, from left to right, John and Richard Moore, Walter Chase, unidentified, and Robert Chase. (Courtesy of Larry Chase.)

Boy Scouts march in the 1942 Memorial Day parade (above) and gather for a troop photograph in 1955 (below). Wilmington has seen multiple Boy Scout troops over the decades, and scouting has remained a popular activity for young boys in the area, with troops forming soon after the creation of the Boy Scouts of America in 1910 and continuing to the present day. In 1943, Troop 46 was provided with an old sugar house by Martin Brown. Working hard to fix it, the troop made the sugar house its first permanent camp, staying for seven nights to celebrate its completion. Self-supporting during World War II, the troop collected scrap iron and paper to help the war effort and finance camping trips. Girl Scouts also became another popular activity for Wilmington's youth, with troops beginning to form in the 1960s and continuing on today.

Five

WHAT WOULD WE
DO WITHOUT . . . ?

Electricity debuted in the village in 1894. Local blacksmith Joseph Courtemanche decided it was time to replace kerosene streetlamps with electric lights. During a special meeting, voters approved the installation of streetlamps in the village, with service running until 11:00 p.m. and homeowners paying for their own electrical installations. In 1930, New England Power Company bought the Courtemanche electric plant. (Courtesy of the Porter Thayer Collection.)

Above, retired telephone workers, seen with town officials, are being honored in 1958. Below are the old Telephone Exchange buildings. Telephone service first appeared in Wilmington on November 5, 1895, when the New England Company opened service there. At first, the switchboard would be installed at the home of the current exchange agent in town, until offices were rented in 1910. The Central Operator was responsible for answering the phone and connecting the caller to the person they wished to speak with. As time went on, more operators were hired and shifts were taken to run the board 24 hours per day. When switchboards began to be phased out, many felt that a human touch had been lost as the brief exchanges of pleasantries and chit-chat with the operators were now gone. (Above, courtesy of the Brattleboro Historical Society.)

The village of Wilmington's water supply flows from several springs on Haystack Mountain. By 1904, the water was piped into homes, businesses, and hydrants around the village, providing quality water. A reservoir on Ray Hill (shown here in 1912) was built for water storage, while today it is stored in an underground storage tank. In 1923, the Village Water Works was established and still maintains the water supply today.

Prior to the flooding of Harriman Reservoir in 1924, New England Power Company moved cemeteries to higher ground. Riverview Cemetery had a designated area for some of the graves. Others were moved to Intervale and Boyd Cemeteries. Shown here are steps from Beaver Street leading to Restland Cemetery. Old records indicate this cemetery location was once the Congregational churchyard. The Averell Cemetery, east of town, dates back to the mid-1700s.

Wilmington's rural demographics made for a prime location for a private hospital (shown here). After arriving in town, Dr. Herman Walker saw the need for a hospital and opened one on East Main Street in 1939. In 1942, the thriving practice was temporarily closed so Walker could serve with the US Coast Guard. After only a year he was released from service in order to reopen the hospital.

With no pagers or cell phones, the fire department depended on the "red phone" to alert them of a fire. Pictured are Leon and Florence Covey receiving an award for their dedication to public service by answering the phone 24/7 from 1958 to 1970. Until 1970, Covey also ran an ambulance service transporting those who needed emergency care. The ambulance service was run in conjunction with Covey's funeral business.

In 1917, in response to increased automobile traffic, Wilmington erected a traffic post in the center of town in order to help safely control traffic. Constable Earl Streeter stood at the post for a week until drivers became accustomed to the new traffic regulations devised to reduce accidents. After an incident of vandalism in the spring of 1948, the village trustees met with the town selectmen and formed a police patrol later that summer. It was decided to have the town constable increase the number of special officers and patrol the street each evening. The expenses were shared by both the village and the town. Wilmington continued to have constables until the late 1960s. Fred Look, pictured here during Old Home Week 1960, served as first constable from 1959 until 1969, at which point Wilmington transitioned to a police department.

The Wilmington Fire Department is pictured here in 1958. Before purchasing a gasoline-powered fire truck and forming a fire department in 1931, hand-drawn pumper and hose carts were used to fight fires. The Methodist church bell would sound the alarm, and everyone available would pull the carts, using underground cisterns as a water supply. Hydrants were installed in 1905, and later a whistle was placed at Parmelee & Howe to alert the firemen.

The street commissioner maintained Wilmington's streets. Men were hired, with or without horse teams, for breaking roads, bridge construction, and brush cutting. Records show that in 1874, a "Mr. Brown" was paid $6 for five days work cutting ice on the highway. Town assets for 1911 included three snow rollers. After the 1938 flood, this large, modified boiler was used as a culvert on Stowe Hill Road. (Courtesy of Linda Olsson.)

Six

COUNTRY LEISURE

Wilmington's Forest & Stream Club was formed in 1892, eventually occupying 500 acres of land. Sixty members contributed, receiving the right to hunt, fish, and enjoy other outdoor sports and recreation at the club's three-story clubhouse and cottages. Among the many honored guests were former presidents Rutherford B. Hayes and Grover Cleveland. Having succumbed to fires and financial woes, the Chimney Hill Association eventually bought the land in the 1960s.

Alice Newton (right) rows her canoe on Lake Raponda in 1930 with an unidentified companion. Newton's grandfather Moses Newton was involved with the construction of the original Hotel Raponda in 1889. Newton's parents, Herbert B. and Katherine Newton (daughter of O.O. Ware), owned a cottage at the lake that was once used as the icehouse for the hotel. (Courtesy of the Newton family.)

A descendant of Martin Brown rides a homemade float known as a "Hot Dog" at Lake Raponda in the early 1950s. In 1949, the town selectmen proposed a contest to name the public beach at the lake. A total of 34 children entered the contest, which was won by Carl Brown. Brown's winning entry was "Green Mountain Beach," the name that is still used today. (Courtesy of Judy Hodgman.)

Over the years, many have flocked to Lake Raponda in search of a quiet respite. Originally known as the Great Lake, it was later named Ray Pond, after owners William and Benjamin Ray. The name eventually evolved into Lake Raponda. The lake was purchased along with two mills in 1788; the mills were demolished to increase the size of the dam, which in turn enlarged the lake. The lake later became popular with tourists, and families from out of state traveled by train to vacation at the lake during the summer. Booming tourism supported the creation of the Hotel Raponda in 1889. Among the guests that first season were Rudyard Kipling and Theodore Roosevelt. After burning in 1896, a replacement (pictured here) was built by H.W. Stearns and opened in 1900. While the hotel no longer exists, Lake Raponda remains popular with both locals and visitors alike.

Memorial Hall was built in 1902 and became a social center of Wilmington, offering showings of locally produced plays (above) and later films. Plays were performed by local adults and students and, for many years, featured a painted stage curtain (below). The original curtain featured a painting with a view from the bottom of Lisle Hill. The painting depicted the center of town, including the original wooden Parmelee & Howe building. By the 1940s, movies were being shown for 20¢ per viewing. Films were often preceded by newsreels about World War II or cartoons, and silent films were accompanied by a live pianist. Popular films of the time included *Three Stooges* films, *Lassie* movies, and westerns featuring Gene Autry and Roy Rogers.

Childs Tavern was originally built in 1898. It was designed by the same New York architectural firm that designed Memorial Hall. The original owners built the tavern after deciding they had outgrown their other property, the Vermont House. The hotel kept the name Childs Tavern until the property was sold to Floyd Crafts Sr. in 1911. After some renovations, the building was renamed the Crafts Inn, the name it retains today. Folks from the city would frequently travel by train to Wilmington and stay at the hotel for months at a time, finding respite from the hustle and bustle of city life. The front porch, with its large rocking chairs, was an extremely popular spot for guests during the hotel's heyday. While ownership has changed over the years, the hotel has remained a fixture in Wilmington up to the present day.

Not to be confused with the ski area, Haystack Mountain is named for its sharp, pointed summit cone that rises to 3,462 feet. The subject of local history, myth, legend, and lore that includes vanishing hikers, a "bottomless" summit lake, and a lost cave, it once hosted a fire tower during the 1920s (pictured). Haystack offers great hiking opportunities, including the Ridge Trail that connects Haystack with Mount Snow.

These quaint cabins were the result of increased automobile travel along the Molly Stark Trail running through Wilmington, which later became Route 9. The trail was paved in 1936, making for ideal scenic tours of southern Vermont, and the need for accommodations grew. Walter and Ruby Streeter opened the Haystack Cabins west of the village in the late 1930s. There were 14 cabins, a dining room, and a gift shop.

Local Shell filling station owner Kenny Rafuse had a passion for baseball, even though he did not play. Shown here is a team sponsored by Rafuse, one of the many town ball teams. Sunday afternoon ball games were extremely popular for both players and spectators. Neighborhood kids started playing at a young age and ball fields popped up all over town, including one located where the firehouse was later built.

The grandstand at Wilmington Central School, built in 1915, is seen here on Labor Day of that year. Baseball was an especially popular attraction, and the large grandstand provided shaded seating for spectators attending from around the valley. At the bottom was a small window where Wilmington resident Fred Poupart sold hamburgers, hot dogs, and sodas. Repaired after the 1938 flood, the grandstand was used until 1970.

UNITED STATES OF AMERICA.

NUMBER
126

$100

STATE OF VERMONT

Wilmington Country Club
Inc.

SIX PER CENT SINKING FUND
GOLD BOND

AUTHORIZED ISSUE $50,000.

Wilmington Country Club, Inc., a Vermont corporation (hereinafter called the "CLUB"), for value received, promises to pay to the bearer or, in case of registration, to the registered holder hereof, the sum of

ONE HUNDRED DOLLARS

In 1929, the Wilmington Country Club was opened. The club was created by Martin Brown and a small group of local men who wished to have a golf course in Wilmington. The nine-hole course was designed by Ralph Barton, who had previously designed the golf course at Yale. Touted for its view of Haystack Mountain and the surrounding countryside, the Wilmington Country Club included several holes copied from famous courses around the world.

Camp Najerog was a short distance off the Molly Stark Trail and bordered Lake Raponda. Located on the 270-acre Harold Gore farm in the pristine Green Mountains, the camp theme was "The Green Mountain Boys." The boys attending camp would spend eight weeks experiencing farm life, while also enjoying camp activities like boating and horseback riding. The camp ran from 1924 to 1970. (Courtesy of Sally Gore.)

The Wilmington Flying Club, founded in 1950, consisted of eight members, including Stanly Carner (left) and Andy Crawford (right). The group purchased a 1946 Aeronca Champion and housed it on the Aldrich farm. After the group sold their plane and disbanded in 1955, Carner built a hanger on his Ray Hill property, and both he and Crawford bought planes. Their Ray Hill runway totaled 1,725 feet and became very active after the development of Mount Snow. Carner's field was included on the FAA Bureau of Aeronautics map and a field number was assigned by the State Aeronautics Department. Both men experienced their share of mishaps. Once, a horrific wind came up and destroyed Carner's hanger, twisting up his plane. Another time, Crawford ran into a heavy fog and had to make an emergency landing in deep snow. Crawford, known as the daredevil of the two, also flew several search and rescue missions with the Civil Air Patrol, while Carner, known as the "Flying Milkman," was a bush pilot who could land on any surface. (Courtesy of Isabelle Hadley.)

When Parmelee & Howe was rebuilt in 1931 after burning down earlier that year, the new structure was outfitted with a brand-new ice cream and soda fountain. The soda fountain was a hit with Wilmington youth who enjoyed grabbing ice cream, candy, and snacks before catching a play or film at Memorial Hall. The fountain was removed in 1969. (Courtesy of Judy Hodgman.)

An evening out during the summer in the 1950s and early 1960s might have meant dancing at Pinkham's Barn on Stowe Hill. The well-attended square, round, and polka dances proved to be a great hit, attracting many for a night out. In the late 1960s, the barn became known as the Twin Silos, the largest fully licensed night club in the Mount Snow Valley.

Before the large ski areas started operating, kids were known to ski up and down the streets while hanging onto ropes attached to a horse. Later came the small rope tows, like the one behind the Ray property on West Main Street. In 1946, Hogback Ski Area opened, followed by Mount Snow in 1954 and Haystack Ski Area in 1964. This was the beginning of ski tourism in the area, with inns, lodges, and ski shops popping up throughout the valley. To accommodate the growing sport, Clapp's Sporting Goods from Brattleboro opened a sister store in Wilmington, next door to the Old Red Mill, supplying skiers with the latest ski equipment for rent or for sale. Stanly Carner is shown below transporting ski equipment to Mount Snow for the weekly student ski program. (Both, courtesy of the Brattleboro Historical Society.)

Albert and Louise Brissette enjoyed bowling in Brattleboro in the early 1950s and took great interest in the sport. They soon decided to pursue the business of bowling locally. After much research, and partnering with Verne and Kay Boyd, they brought bowling to Wilmington. Senior town selectman Fred Thomas, shown here at the grand opening of B & B Bowling in the fall of 1961 (center), bowled the very first ball. Owners Boyd (far left) and Brissette (far right) flank selectmen Porter Farwell and Leonard Brown during the widely attended opening. The nine-lane candlepin bowling alley proved to be a great attraction for all ages. Weeknight leagues were formed and open bowling was popular on the weekend. The name changed to North Star Bowl after a new partnership was formed between the Brissettes and Ken and Anne Hopkins. (Courtesy of the Brattleboro Historical Society.)

Seven

THE PEOPLE

Joan Newton Cuneo, the daughter of John Newton, of the Newton Brothers, was known as one of the first women to drive race cars in the United States. One of the greatest attractions during Old Home Week 1910 was Cuneo racing her Knox car through town, reaching 72 miles per hour! She is shown here on another occasion giving rides through the center of Wilmington.

Pictured in 1947 is the Barber family. From left to right are (first row) children Janet and Muriel; (second row) Minnie, Merton, and grandmother Clara Barber. Merton Barber was a member of Wilmington High School's first graduating class in 1902 and was a state representative for southern Vermont, serving in congress in Montpelier for many years, with three terms in the House and two in the Senate. The Barber homestead (pictured), believed to be one of the first houses built in Mill Hollow, was acquired by the family in 1902. In the early 1930s, Merton had the back porch enclosed in order to start a business making and selling maple candy to O.O. Ware's store. In 2003, the home was sold to the Historical Society of Wilmington by Barber's daughter Muriel as a place to display Wilmington history.

Ralph Medbury stands before H.F. Barber & Son Store (now the town offices), which he ran for many years. Medbury was an active member of the Wilmington community and an avid photographer, documenting many Wilmington events. Some of his photographs even appear in this book. In particular, Medbury photographed local servicemen and women in uniform when they were home on leave and displayed these photographs in his store.

Ethel Courtemanche Strawser plays the organ at the age of 101. Strawser taught music for 27 years in the Wilmington school system and was credited with founding the high school band. As a young girl, she watched as streetlamps were filled with kerosene in the morning by a man who then returned at night to light them. Her father made the move to provide Wilmington with electricity.

A milk wagon is pictured in the Old Home Week 1950 parade, painted and lettered by Eleoda "Leo" Maynard. Maynard spent time in Burlington learning the art of sign lettering and painted many signs around Wilmington, including the scroll of Wilmington's World War II veterans that stood on the corner by Parmelee & Howe. Maynard lettered this Carner's Jersey Milk wagon for the sum of $21.

Guy Hawkins is often remembered for his speech during Old Home Week 1950. In 1928, Hawkins assumed the position of woods manager at the New England Box Company's factory, which had just begun operations in Wilmington. Hawkins was active in town affairs, including as director of the Civilian Defense during World War II. The Guy Hawkins Foundation was established after his passing in 1979.

Clinton Hall had a passion for baseball; he is shown here by the grandstand during practice with the town team. Destroyed by the 1938 flood, the grandstand was rebuilt with Hall's help. Hall served as a representative in Montpelier and was instrumental in the local education system. Hall became Wilmington's very first fire chief in 1931 and later served as postmaster from 1935 to 1958. (Courtesy of Priscilla Lackey.)

In 1912, Arthur Robinson was hired at the Childs Tavern for his interior decorating talents. The job was wallpapering the guest rooms. He went on to become the tavern's full-time handyman, tended to the horses, and was even a chef when needed. Later, he became custodian at the Wilmington Central School. Robinson had a talent for building instruments; his favorite was the violin. Robinson is shown here with one of his masterpieces.

William Pool (left) and Leon Covey (right) worked together for many years at Covey & Allen Funeral Home (see page 58 for the history of the business). Pool, a veteran of the Battle of the Bulge, was an avid wildlife photographer, farmer, and past Master of the Victory Grange. A locally active 32nd degree Mason, Pool was also extremely involved with Masonic functions at the Vermont state level. He even served as a C.C. Haynes trustee and a town lister. Pool was a devoted friend to many, and he was always willing to lend a helping hand, and not for the recognition. Covey was a funeral director for over 50 years and a member of Social Lodge No. 38 F&AM. Covey served Wilmington as a cemetery commissioner and a village trustee. Both men were well-respected citizens who worked graciously together serving families around the area during difficult times.

Principal, educator, coach, and longtime friend, Newton Baker was an icon in the Wilmington school system. Baker's career in education started in Wilmington while he was the principal. Baker coached field hockey, baseball, and basketball, inspiring his nickname "Coach." The boys' basketball team became well-known throughout the region and went to state tournaments thanks to Baker, who is pictured here with the team in 1942.

From left to right, owner Philip Ware, William Pool, and Gerald Jacobs are at the meat counter of O.O. Ware's store. A graduate of Wilmington High, Ware served in the Pacific during World War II. A member of several social lodges and veterans' groups, Ware also served on multiple town boards. He was a semiprofessional photographer and a musician who enjoyed big band and jazz music.

Tag-team Merton Learnard and Wayland Hall, custodians for the Wilmington High School, worked side-by-side for many years. Learnard (pictured here) was a longtime Wilmington resident and graduate of Wilmington High School. After graduation, he joined the Air Force, serving in India during World War II as a staff sergeant. Learnard earned several medals, including the Good Conduct Medal and the Victory Medal. After the service, he returned home to Wilmington and went to work at the high school. While working as a custodian, Learnard was certain to give an orange to every student at Christmastime. He had a passion for helping others and was a true people person. Hall, his coworker, resided in Wilmington for 21 years directly across the street from Learnard's residence. Both men went on to retire from the high school having made a great team, keeping the school immaculate for many years.

Leonard "Pete" Johnson (left) and Ralph Howe Jr. (right) ran Parmelee & Howe from 1951 until its closing in 1994. Johnson, a flight officer for the Army Air Corps, flew B-26 aircraft during World War II. Whenever Johnson flew over Wilmington, schoolchildren rushed outside to watch his plane. Johnson was an avid outdoorsman and deeply involved in his community. When he was not hunting in Somerset or salmon fishing in Canada, Johnson served on the school board during the 1950s and as fire chief during the 1960s. He was twice granted the honor of being grand marshal at Old Home Week, including once as co–grand marshal with Howe. Howe, also a veteran, served under General Patton at the Battle of the Bulge. Equally involved in his community, Howe served as a founder and trustee of the Deerfield Valley Health Center, was a member of the Guy Hawkins Fund, and was an administrator of the C.C. Haynes Scholarship Fund. Howe was well-known for his wry wit and humor as well as his ever-present tobacco pipe. (Courtesy of Rev. Ralph W. Howe.)

Born and raised in Wilmington, Evelyn Fitch Keefe became a well-versed Wilmington historian. She attended the Cutting one-room schoolhouse (see page 28) and graduated with the class of 1924 from Wilmington High School. After graduation, Keefe worked as a clerk at the drugstore. The Parmelees were living upstairs at the time, and the way of life was pretty simple back then. Life growing up on the Fitch farm (see page 36) was a joyous time for her, from helping her father to running on the stone walls and playing in the river. A trip to North Adams, Massachusetts, via the Hoot-Toot & Whistle Railroad was a special occasion for Keefe that took days to plan. Homemade ice cream was a delicious treat that she helped to make using ice that had been stored in the icehouse. Keefe was very fond of sharing and documenting memories and Wilmington history with others.

Margaret Covey Greene (left) was born and raised in Wilmington and graduated from Wilmington High School. Later, she became a teacher at the Coldbrook District No. 6 school, then taught third and fifth grades at the Grange building and Wilmington school. Taking great pleasure in teaching children, she taught Sunday school at the Baptist church where she was a member. Greene was also a member of the Mayflower Chapter 19 Order of the Eastern Star and a librarian at Pettee Memorial Library for many years. Greene was instrumental in the historical society and will always be remembered for her knowledge and dedication to organizing and documenting information about Wilmington cemeteries, family genealogy, and newspaper clippings. Rita May Staib and Greene diligently worked on the house project for the society's research records. Shown here talking with Louise Woffenden (right) on the Woffenden farm, Greene enjoyed visiting people and collecting information to preserve for future generations.

Janet Barber Pool, daughter of Merton and Minnie Barber, was a lifelong resident of Wilmington. She worked at the family business, Barber Insurance, eventually purchasing it from her father. While Pool had no children of her own, she was considered "Nana" to many. Here in front of the family business, Pool observes as children enjoy country living. Another local historian, Pool dedicated hours to sharing and preserving her knowledge of Wilmington.

Living to nearly 103, Viola Bishop Morse was very independent from a young age and regularly delivered milk to the creamery on her way to school. After graduating from Wilmington, she became a teacher. After marrying Harry Morse, they purchased a farm together and became dealers for Blue Seal Feeds in 1949. An active member of the Vermont Farm Bureau, Morse was chosen Farm Woman of the Year in 1985.

Eight

EVENTS

George Streeter and E.M. Haynes started manufacturing snow rollers at the Choate Manufacturing Company building in the early 1900s. The rollers, weighing up to 2,500 pounds, were made in two different sizes for four- or six-horse hitches. Rollers were already being used in parts of northern Vermont. Rollers, like the one shown here on Castle Hill, packed snow into a hard surface for sleighs, buggies, wagons, and horses to travel.

Shoveling roads gave way to snow rollers, then bulldozers, and soon graders—but even then, cars needed to use tire chains. Shown here in 1939 are a grader and other vehicles traversing a snow-covered Main Street. The previous January a blizzard hit Wilmington with 21 inches of drifting snow. The storm resulted in one man's death; he was wallowing to work through deep snow. (Courtesy of Linda Olsson.)

In 1935, a group of 23 men came to Wilmington to form a Civilian Conservation Corps camp on land leased from Elwin Haslund near Lake Raponda. When the camp was finished, the group was increased to 200 men. Work included planting trees, building bridges, fighting fires, and eradicating gypsy moths. Many of Vermont's state parks were built or improved by CCC members. Pay was around $30 per month.

Farmers' Day 1919 featured a special appearance by a Curtiss airplane from Boston, Massachusetts. Its passenger, former Wilmington resident Ralph Mann, orchestrated the event, having always dreamed of seeing the town of Wilmington from the air. Mann announced his intentions with a telegram sent a few days before the flight. After arriving in Brattleboro, the pilot, Lieutenant Lee, and Mann had dinner and then proceeded to Wilmington. The craft arrived in Wilmington just 15 minutes later at 2:45 in the afternoon. The craft circled the village several times at an altitude of 4,000 feet. Just before departing, Mann dropped, via a toy parachute, the first piece of airmail ever delivered in Wilmington—a letter addressed to his friend Merton F. Barber. Following the drop, the airplane proceeded directly back to Boston, reaching the city in just under two hours.

Four days of rain in September 1938 unleashed catastrophic flooding in Wilmington. With the storm under way, state highway employees Andrew Crawford and Benjamin Bernard were called to check on a section of highway. Quickly forced to abandon their truck, the men retreated on foot, walking on guardrail cables to stay above the water. Crawford found his home surrounded by rushing water, his wife and children still inside. Using a grader, he attempted to reach them, but it succumbed to the storm (above). Eventually able to rig a rope between the grader and the house, Crawford used the rope to carry his family to safety with help from Lawrence Willard and William Brown. Meanwhile, the Main Street Bridge had collapsed, sagging into the swollen river and severing southern Vermont's main telephone line in the process. (Below, courtesy of Walter White.)

Adamsville Bridge was another casualty of the 1938 flood. Being of similar design to other Wilmington bridges, it was made of wood with tall sides. What is known as Higley Hill Road today once crossed this bridge, going directly through Adams Farm before connecting to present-day Higley Hill Road. During the flood, this bridge was washed out and carried down the river, causing more havoc as it wiped out other bridges on its journey downstream. A new cement bridge was installed upstream, taking a year to complete. In the meantime, traffic was rerouted with vehicles fording the river at a shallow crossing before heading back south to meet up with the road again. The storm responsible for the Great Flood of 1938 remains the only system ever recorded to hit Vermont as a tropical cyclone. Pictured here are Ada and Louis Adams. (Courtesy of Larry Chase.)

The 1938 flood brought waters seven feet high. Many homes and businesses were ravaged. The village and fairgrounds were hit hard, demolishing the grandstands, lifting C.C. Haynes Hall off its foundation stones (pictured) and canceling Farmers' Day. Roads washed out, power lines toppled, and livestock were carried away. Despite the torrent of water, residents across town leapt into action, helping neighbors escape the rising waters. (Courtesy of Linda Olsson.)

August 1939 brought unique entertainment upon Wilmington: a carnival monkey was on the loose! The monkey executed a daring escape from a traveling carnival troupe, causing great excitement. First spotted atop town hall, he swung from roof to roof around the village, eluding capture for several days. Once caught, the monkey was lodged at a home on South Main Street where he entertained visitors daily until the troupe retrieved him.

The World War II–era Aircraft Warning Service, formed in 1941 by the Army Air Force with help from the American Legion, trained citizens to spot and recognize aircraft. Spotters were stationed at observation posts or homes high on hills. Once spotted, sightings were phoned into headquarters. Pictured is Fay Vose, one of Wilmington's spotters. Spotters were recognized for hours of service with pins and certificates.

August 14, 1945, known as V-J Day for Victory Over Japan, brought the message on the radio: Japan had surrendered. The mill whistle blew, church bells rang, and a bonfire was lit. Celebrations continued for days with parades, bands, singing, and dancing in the streets. One year later, a big parade with floats and bands was held to recognize the sacrifices made during the war. (Courtesy of Pat Morris.)

Built in 1820, the original Masonic Lodge was located on the old town common and brought down off the hill in 1837. For years, there was speculation on the whereabouts of this building. While doing research to prepare for his Old Home Week 1950 speech on the history of the old town common, Guy Hawkins discovered an old deed for the building. With tape measure in hand, he measured the building that he suspected was the old lodge. Finding the measurements right to the specifications, Hawkins declared that it was the Bowker Block, next door to the Baptist church, owned by Peter Wimmelman and containing apartments at the time. The first telephone exchange had also been located in this very building. In 1965, the property was purchased by Lincoln Haynes and was once again moved (shown here) to just north of the Old Red Mill, where it is located today. (Courtesy of Deborah Canedy.)

Nine

TRADITIONS

Wilmington has enthusiastically embraced Memorial Day since the holiday was first created in 1868 by order of Gen. John A. Logan of the Grand Army of the Republic. Annual tributes include a parade down Main Street with salutes and wreath-laying by local veterans, memorial services at Memorial Hall, and, until its dissolution, ceremonies conducted by the local C.B. Lawton Post of the Grand Army of the Republic (pictured).

A gift of Civil War veteran A.P. Childs, this Soldiers' Monument was presented to the town on Memorial Day 1897. The monument stood at the base of Lisle Hill and was unveiled with great fanfare. Its inscription read: "In Memory of Our Country's Defenders." Seen here with the monument is a Civil War–era naval gun, which now rests at the site of the original town common on Lisle Hill.

When the small, arched "chapel" atop the original Soldiers' Monument was damaged, it was replaced with a new top-piece bearing the likeness of a Civil War soldier carved from stone. The new version of the monument sat at the base of Lisle Hill until it was eventually moved to the Pettee Memorial Library lawn at some point between 1907 and 1910, where it remains today.

Civil War hero Maj. F.W. Childs commissioned Memorial Hall in 1902 as a tribute to Wilmington's finest. In 1914, Childs unveiled two tablets on either side of the proscenium arch at the hall. These tablets, set in frames of white and gilt, bear the names of 115 Civil War veterans and 75 Revolutionary War veterans—all from Wilmington. The ceremony was attended by people from many surrounding towns and all sat attentively in the flag-draped hall as veterans spoke of their experiences. When Childs eventually sold Memorial Hall to the town in 1921, he stipulated that the tablets as well as the portraits of veterans on the walls must remain, with more portraits being added periodically. He also required that the town hold a memorial service in the hall each year, a tradition that has been honored every Memorial Day since.

Wilmington has been honoring veterans since the Revolutionary War. This wooden World War I honor roll (left) was eventually replaced with a permanent granite stone and plaque bearing the names of those who served along with this inscription: "Dedicated to those who offered their lives in humanity's defense in the war of the nations 1914–1918." It is now located at Pettee Memorial Library. Memorial Day 1944 brought the dedication of another honor roll (below) inscribed with "We Honor Those Who Serve," honoring World War II veterans. The construction was completed by Earl Streeter, with the design, lettering, and painting done by Eleoda Maynard. This honor roll stood in the village center for several years until two permanent bronze plaques were placed at the school. These plaques also include the names of veterans who served in the Korean Conflict.

The 1940 Farmers' Day Fair is seen here in full swing. Wilmington has had a long and celebrated tradition of fairs, dating back to the town's agricultural boom in the mid-1800s. In the 19th century, the Wilmington Agricultural Society held what were then called "exhibits" to display fruits, vegetables, livestock, and crafts. Many of these displays were set up at Memorial Hall during the early years. Being primarily a farming town, many townspeople were proud to display the results of their hard work. Many businesses even took part in displaying well-crafted tools and products in which they took pride. These exhibits went on until at least 1894, around which time the Victory Grange began putting on exhibits for a few years. The first official "fairs" began in the early 20th century and have occurred nearly every year since, being cancelled only a few times due to wars and floods.

Early fairs were marked by a friendly rivalry between the north of Wilmington and the east. The two factions competed to see who could assemble the largest team of oxen. Fairs were heavily focused on exhibiting agricultural products, with awards issued to all manner of fruits, vegetables, grains, livestock, homemade foods, and crafts, including doilies, aprons, pin cushions, quilts, and even underwear! For years, baseball games were incredibly popular events, with games held

every afternoon. Horse-pulls were also popular sights. Farmers and loggers brought their horses from surrounding towns to see which team could haul the heaviest load. Attendees could sample homemade ice cream, donuts, or cider while wandering the exhibit halls displaying crafts, fresh pies, or livestock. Above is a view of the 1915 fair, a year when extra judges had to be procured for the apple judging competition!

The first Reunion of the Sons and Daughters of the Town of Wilmington, held in July 1890, was the beginning of a decennial tradition still in existence today. A simple family reunion turned into an elaborate community event for all to enjoy after it was decided to open the invitation to everyone. Returning guests were welcomed by four American flags that adorned the main streets. Each had a motto or sentiment on both sides like "Should Old Acquaintance be Forgot?," "Home of Our Childhood," "Welcome Old-Timers," "Home Again," and "Hurrah for Wilmington." The celebration continued for days with returning guests visiting Mount Haystack, Lake Raponda, and the old schoolhouse.

The reunion's grand parade in 1900 was likely the largest parade attempted in the county. The Forest & Stream Club was well-represented with six floats pulled by beautiful teams of horses (shown here). Other events included a concert and dance under the big tent and then supper and dancing at the Vermont House until the wee hours on Friday night.

The August 1910 reunion exercises started on a Tuesday evening at Memorial Hall. A paper written by Charles H. Parmelee entitled "Some Changes of the Past Decade" was read, and 200 stereopticon portraits were presented by C.M. Russell. Thursday afternoon a campfire and music were provided outside Memorial Hall before a special train ride on the Hoot-Toot & Whistle Railroad that evening.

For the fourth reunion in 1920 there were 500 visiting guests registered at Memorial Hall on Friday evening. Each day had a different theme: Friday was Soldiers' and Sailors' Day, Saturday was Farmers' Day, Monday was Bennington Day, Tuesday was Banquet Day, and Wednesday was Picnic Day. A large steer furnished by Beaver Brook, Inc., was cooked, serving an estimated 1,500 guests just in time for the baseball game.

The Old Home Week 1930 parade extended over a mile, with automobiles and floats competing for prizes. First place went to the "Old Timers" from Beaver Brook, and second place went to a "Sunflower" decorated automobile driven by Alice Courtemanche. Memorial Hall was host to a concert and dance. Special services were held Sunday morning for the 150th anniversary of the First Congregational Church in town.

The dedication of the Newton H. Baker Recreation Field was held on opening day of the 1940 reunion. Following the dedication, the high school alumni, led by the school's band (pictured here), marched from the school to the Old Red Mill, where a banquet was served. On Saturday evening a special "Golden Jubilee" banquet was held at the Congregational church for those who had attended the first reunion of 1890.

For the 1950 reunion, an "Alumni" banquet was held at Childs Tavern, followed by a grand ball. The following day a formal dedication of the old town common plot of land, donated by Martin A. Brown, was the focal point of the reunion. Attendees gathered at the old town common (shown here) to hear Guy Hawkins' historical address.

The Old Home Week 1960 parade heads through the center of town. The Clover Farm store is shown in the background, buntings adorn the town hall, and spectators watch as this miniature team of horses makes its way through town. The award for Best Representation went to Camp Najerog. Later in the day, a dedication ceremony was held at the newly built Wilmington Post Office, followed by a tour of the facilities. Crafts Inn was the location of the "Old Timers" banquet, with nearly 300 attending. A largely attended barn dance was held at the Pinkham farm on Saturday evening.

Ten

THE OUTSKIRTS

In the late 1800s, sisters Cecilia and Mary Heather purchased the old Grimes Place, a 300-acre farm just over the town line in Searsburg. They built a mansion resembling a Scottish manor with 20 elaborate rooms; it was known as the Heather Mansion. The ballroom, situated on the third floor, held many grand concerts during the sisters' ownership. After the sisters sold the mansion, it became the Chateau Inn.

District No. 7 school was known as the Medburyville schoolhouse. The district, organized in 1848 with 10 families living there, was referred to as Medburyville after members of the Medbury family, who were among the first settlers there. Viola Bishop Morse and Margaret Greene, both longtime residents of Wilmington, attended this school. After closing in 1925, the building was converted into a cottage (below). Being a good distance from the village, residents of Medburyville looked after their own needs, and the schoolhouse was used not just for school but also community events. Farmer George Covey was a spokesperson for the area, even acting as an unofficial storekeeper by buying large amounts of food and goods on trips to Brattleboro and selling them to his neighbors to help them avoid long trips to town. (Above, courtesy of Lenny Chapman.)

In the spring, logs had been shipped to the mills so horse teams headed home following a long winter deep in the woods. The horses hauled the logs on skids to the landing where they were stockpiled for the spring river drives. Shown here, several teams make their way along the narrow dirt road through Wilmington to Colrain, Massachusetts, to spend the summer working. Note the schoolhouse in background.

Bordering the fringes of Wilmington and Marlboro is Molly Stark State Park and Mount Olga. In the 1930s, the Civilian Conservation Corps constructed a picnic area here. One hundred more acres were donated in 1939. Later that same year, another 48 acres were donated by Olga Haslund, Mount Olga's namesake. By 1960, a campground had been established, attracting passing motorists ever since. Pictured here is the Mount Olga fire tower.

Not many can say they have lived in three different towns while never moving, though several families living on what is now known as the Handle Road experienced just that. One example is Truman Moore, who purchased 24 acres of land within the township of Somerset in 1842, which eventually became known as the Hermitage. The land and the original house sat within Somerset until 1858, at which point the land was offered to Dover as part of a larger parcel occupied by multiple families. After Dover declined the land, it was transferred to the township of Wilmington. The property became known as the Handle Road and remained in Wilmington until 1870, when Dover finally took over the land. Along with the land, Dover also received two one-room schools and eight miles of road from Wilmington. Shown here is one of those schools, the Bogle School. This school served District No. 2 in Somerset, District No. 16 in Wilmington, and finally District No. 9 in Dover. (Courtesy of Robert Edwards.)

About the Historical Society of Wilmington

The Historical Society of Wilmington is a duly organized nonprofit entity dedicated to collecting, preserving, teaching, and displaying the history of Wilmington, Vermont. The society is an independent group of volunteers that is funded by donations, memberships, and fundraisers.

In 1975, a group of dedicated volunteers saw the need to preserve Wilmington's history, so the Historical Society of Wilmington was established. On June 10, 1975, the first meeting was held at Bissell Parish House. In September, a charter and bylaws were adopted, and officers were elected in October. At first there was no museum or storage space where the society could store artifacts and hold meetings or functions. So items were stored in the Masonic safe, Pettee Memorial Library, and at members' homes. Finally, after many years and research of several structures, the society found a building they could call home.

In 2003, with the guidance and determination of society president Peter Morris, the Barber House at Five Lisle Hill Road (c. 1806) was purchased from Muriel Barber Manning. The Barbers were an important part of Wilmington, so the building came with a lot of history. Merton Barber, Muriel's father, owned and operated a store where the town clerk's office is located—this was known as the Barber Block. Merton was very active in town affairs, and he served three terms in the Vermont House of Representatives as well as two in the Senate. His older daughter, Janet Barber Pool, had a wealth of knowledge about Wilmington history and was an active member of the society at the time of her passing. With the support and dedication from active and non-active members, the museum has come a long way over the past 17 years.

The museum is open during the summer months from the Fourth of July through Labor Day weekend and by appointment as requested. For more information, please call (802) 464-0200 or visit www.WilmingtonHistoricalSociety.com.

Marking our 45th year of dedication to preserving Wilmington's history, we would like to take this opportunity to thank everyone for their continued support of the society.

DISCOVER THOUSANDS OF LOCAL HISTORY BOOKS FEATURING MILLIONS OF VINTAGE IMAGES

Arcadia Publishing, the leading local history publisher in the United States, is committed to making history accessible and meaningful through publishing books that celebrate and preserve the heritage of America's people and places.

Find more books like this at
www.arcadiapublishing.com

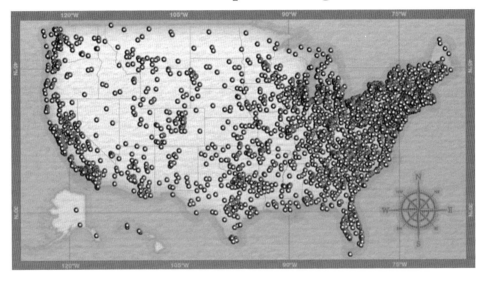

Search for your hometown history, your old stomping grounds, and even your favorite sports team.

Consistent with our mission to preserve history on a local level, this book was printed in South Carolina on American-made paper and manufactured entirely in the United States. Products carrying the accredited Forest Stewardship Council (FSC) label are printed on 100 percent FSC-certified paper.

MADE IN THE USA